MERCY

Róisín Kelly was born in west Belfast and raised in the rural Irish county of Leitrim. After a year as a handweaver on Clare Island and a Masters in Writing at NUI Galway, she now calls Cork City home. Her first chapbook of poetry, *Rapture*, was published by Southword Editions in 2016. Publications in which her work has appeared in Ireland, the US and UK include *Poetry*, *Magma*, *Ambit*, *The Stinging Fly*, *Poetry Ireland Review* and *Winter Papers*. In 2017 she won the Fish Poetry Prize. Her first full-length collection, *Mercy*, was published by Bloodaxe in 2020.

Róisín Kelly

MERCY

BLOODAXE BOOKS

ISBN: 978 1 78037 500 7

First published 2020 by
Bloodaxe Books Ltd,
Eastburn,
South Park,
Hexham,
Northumberland NE46 1BS.

www.bloodaxebooks.com
For further information about Bloodaxe titles
please visit our website and join our mailing list
or write to the above address for a catalogue

Supported using public funding by
**ARTS COUNCIL
ENGLAND**

MIX
Paper from
responsible sources
FSC® C007785

Cover design: Neil Astley & Pamela Robertson-Pearce.

Printed in Great Britain by Bell & Bain Limited, Glasgow, Scotland, on
acid-free paper sourced from mills with FSC chain of custody certification.

for Muireann and Ruth

Καληνύχτα λοιπ όν
βλέπ ω σωρούς π εφτάστερα να σας λικνίζουν τα όνειρα
αλλά εγώ κρατώ στα δάχτυλά
μου τη μουσική για μια καλύτερη μέρα

Kalinihta lipon,
Vlepo sorous peftastera na sas liknizoun ta onira
alla ego krato sta daktila
mou ti (no a) mousiki ya mia kaliteri mera.

And so, goodnight.
I see shooting stars rocking your dreams
but I hold in my fingers
the music for a better day.

NIKOS GATSOS, from *Amorgos*
tr. Joanna Eleftheriou

ACKNOWLEDGEMENTS

Acknowledgements are due to the editors of the following publications where some of these poems first appeared: *Ambit, Blunderbuss, Fish Anthology 2017, Headstuff, The Irish Times, Magma, Mascara Literary Review* (Australia), *Poetry* (USA), *The Stinging Fly, Winter Papers* volume 3 (Curlew Editions, 2017).

Seven of the poems were published in a pamphlet, *Rapture* (Southword Editions, 2016), and Bloodaxe Books wishes to thank Munster Literature Centre for its support.

Deep gratitude and affection are owed to the following people and organisations who have been there for me throughout the writing and editing of *Mercy*: My parents Mairéad and Peter, and their partners Eamonn and Marcella; Neil Astley and the staff at Bloodaxe; Maureen Kennelly and the staff at Poetry Ireland; The Arts Council for a Travel and Training Award that enabled me to attend writing workshops on the island of Thásos in Greece in 2017, where I benefited from the expert guidance of poet Aimee Nezhukumatathil (with additional thanks to faculty Christopher Bakken and Allison Wilkins, and especially to Joanna Eleftheriou who kindly translated the segment of Nikos Gatsos' *Amorgos* in the epigraph); Rachel Parry and Cormac Boydell of the Beara Peninsula for their warmth and hospitality during my residency there in 2019, as well as Marc O'Sullivan Vallig and the staff at the Beara Arts Festival; writer Zsuzsi Gartner; and finally to all the people in or on Belfast, Mohill, Clare Island, Galway and Cork who have ever made for me a home.

CONTENTS

Mercy

On the beach, I undress in the dark.
Naked and blind before the gods, below too many stars.

Here is my body, which I was told to never touch.
An Orthodox shrine glows red by the closed coffee truck.

But as the Aegean comes to my hips, rises within me,
my movements stir luminous plankton or algae:

bright opal specks in the water
that drift from my wrists, around my cold breasts.

They glow and swirl and die like shooting stars,
turned on by my nakedness. They are kind.

I didn't think such tiny compassion
could make me want to cry. How gorgeous

they are, mysterious creatures
dazzling the same seas that Homer once looked on,

that surrounded the ancient Greeks on all sides.
When I begin to walk back, I will hide

from the twin suns of any car I hear coming:
all women learn to be shadows, crouching

down low in the pines. Artemis, I can turn only to you
in a world with such dim light to live by.

Give me the flight of deer through the woods,
fleeing the hunters' sharp spears.

Help me decipher these sparkling trails
like the Milky Way's dust in Morse code.

Guide the small boat of my body back to my self.
Tell me which path brings me home.

Leave

You are leaving, as the others did in turn,
after they took what worth there was
from the time we had together. Here is the fallen
apple's flesh fading to a winter sunset's pale red.
Here is the separation of seed from core,
the slow return to earth. What happens
down there in the black soil, what dream
of the frozen world? I believe
there is something still alive that waits,
sweetening in its fermentation, in its nourishing
of an earth that returns again and again
fruit rounded in its wholeness. In our hands
we cup apples like memories, bend to taste
what seems the same juice, the same sugars,
that remind us the sun will rise after night,
the birds will sing after winter. I watch your plane
ascend at dusk and play the scene
backwards on a loop, so that you do not fly
but fall, returning and returning to me.
But I will let you go, for only then
can the seed you leave rise like a cold star
to my heart. In years to come, I will search the sky
for you, whose sugared constellations are a trail
towards another world in which we'll meet again.
For now, the runway stretches into darkness.
In the cellars, barrelled apples sleep
and dream their short lives in reverse.

Mars in Retrograde

June comes to the sky above Leitrim
and Mars is as red as a rose.

Our garden's roses stare longingly upwards,
this heat is killing them.

Oh Plough, slip some water
from your tilting pan to my poor roses,

into the red mouth of Mars.
The swinging bench moans like a ship

all around me, and I am adrift
in a sea of stars.

Cut me loose from this rope of fairy lights
entwined like a glittering snake

around the chains and the boards.
Let me float to Orion,

let my fingers find his belt's cold buckle.
Oh Mars, my love with red hair

is gone from me and in your single,
maddened eye, I have glimpsed

the men I'll sacrifice to follow him.
I have seen the future slipping from me

like a lonely satellite. I
have heard the creaking of a thousand

ships released at once
like a breath across the face of Earth.

Tom Barry

Gold stars above Leitrim's cut fields
were almost enough, once.
But last week in Tesco I heard a cry
that was my baby, my baby.

Once I wore a rainbow scarf
and every shop-front lit up for me.
My eyes once held the warning glow
of red Atlantic bulbs:

the breakfast table of love
has wrecked many ships.
Saturn's rings, an empty attic room,
dust motes in sunlight.

The only truth worth knowing:
that we are alone.
The moon rises and something in me rises with it
like a howl.

I dip my hands between my legs
and streak my face with red.
Dust I am, and to dust I will return –
in a starless dusk I lie in the grass with my gun.

I long for a man between my lips,
for my eyes to reflect two Jupiters at the last.
Waiting for the lonely whistle-blast,
the light at the bend,

I see the train fly backwards over silver sleepers
as apple peel flies upwards to my silver knife.

Chameleon

I am the Lizard Queen!

LISA SIMPSON

In bed last night
with my real self I lay chillin.

Opal vein mined
from no dark Andamooka hunk.

The price of rainbow
is the body's shell, split.

Adaptation no more, bitch.
Out she comes

like the lizard men
sheddin their humanskin.

Carved in luminous
like the fine jade bra

that stunned
when he tore her open.

Trees makin a cathedral
of absence

neon signs like green moons
in their aisles.

Welcome was
the knife in her back

on the steps to Montmartre
cos a long road is life

if you never becomin
the creach that is nothin

& everthin. Like glass.
Like the lobster

translucent as ice
fisherboy netted in Maine.

Little goddess, tidewitch
he returned to the waves.

Because she female.
Because she strange. Rare

          as blue amber
seadaughter   shadowself
          eggcarrier

Penelope

In a tongue that still belongs to me – despite everything –
I try to name it, his little boat. *Bád beag Stamatis.*

But for the dried coral and starfish, for his sharp knife,
I have no words, nor for how sunlight in the evening

panels the water, or for how the island from here is all
stone and scrub. I can't even name the ocean's colour

in English, that shimmer between turquoise and teal.
As Stamatis begins to cast his nets, one brown foot braced

on the tiller, I pour some wine to the waves and think,
How free I am. I could stay at sea for seven years

and never dream of coming home in any language.
Stamatis, who speaks only Greek, gives me more wine.

Tonight he'll dance while the rest of us kneel on the terrace,
clapping in time. His son will throw a plate at his feet.

Iannis, a delicate glass. The waiters will give me ouzo
and shots of tequila, with rinds of orange to suck and sugar

to lick from my hand. I will tuck my shirt into my bra
and run around barefoot where glass has been broken.

Tomorrow will bring the worst hangover of my life.
For now, sunset spills its gold rings as the prow splits

the sea's warp of silk. My feet are bare on the boards,
my hair gives itself to salt and the wind, as I am carried home

subdued and happy, like a new wife.

Domínio Vale do Mondego

You beat the branches with a stick, so that olives fall
as quickly as the days are passing.

Every night at the press: the smell of crushed olives
like warm darkness you could eat.

Here they eat their bread with olive oil and salt.
At dawn the olive nets are glittering with frost.

The harvest must be in before the solstice,
your flock of sheep must be in before the night.

The terraces in this valley are ancient.
Pine needles make quiet the old Roman road.

When I close my eyes all I see is olives, falling.
And you, bending to pick up a lamb

just as the pink terraces of dusk begin to fade.
A shepherd, a farmer, efficient and practical man.

More than anyone, you know how an hour
has no meaning: there is only a sheep's bell

ringing out the distance between ye, and the time left
in which you can follow it. In this village

of shawled widows, who might they call *witch*?
At the river I write your name on an apple

that I cast into water as black as your name.
Turbines pause in turning on the mountain,

each red lamp burning on a trinity of blades.
Above the Spanish border, a hawk is drifting – forever.

Olives rise from nets and hover mid-air.
Now: is it day? Is it night? It is neither.

The air is a pure colour.

Guarda

You can't start the van at first
even as we're rolling down the hill.

> The valley rises to us
> in the windscreen, an afterlife in green –

you hit the brakes, and still
I continue to fall.

> Then the engine shakes to life
> our metal frame

and the digits of the dashboard clock
stop flickering from 14:12

> to 14:13 and back again
> but become as steady as a flame.

Through hairpin bends
the quarter hour is marked by church bells

> and the reservoir's level of water
> is lower than it has been for years.

Flying above that grey city of dam
the smell of motor oil in the van

> stirs in me I don't know what...
> In Guarda, you park across three parking spots

as a black-shawled widow watches
from her stall of wrinkled plums.

> She's suspecting that I might forsake
> the only fires I've ever learned to make

for a valley kingdom's fallen
yellow apples, and a moon that rises

    with the smoke from every farm
    that burns its olive branches in December.

A Massage Room in West Cork

They tell us the massage room is empty
in the farmhouse attached to the pub
so we sleep there, on a narrow wooden bed.

I watch dream-catchers shiver
on the ceiling, listen to you breathing
and people talking loudly in the yard.

All night your arm lies heavy across me
so I won't roll off in my sleep
and an orange crystal lamp keeps soft

the panes of glassy darkness at the window.
Beyond this room: a gentle curve
of quiet country road.

Within this room: the weight of your arm.
Your body moulded to the shape of mine.
Dreams of oil:

lavender, rose, sweet almond.
Of fingers kneading flesh
in the gold dim. Your glistening skin.

Rapture

On the morning you leave, I go into the garden.
The sound of your car fades in the rattle
of raspberry stalks like papery bones.

Here where the woods begin to take over
raspberries grew all summer. I filled bowls and bowls
with them, more than I could ever eat
and the birds went hungry.

Now each dewdrop holds the winter world.
In a glass globe I wait for the berries to ripen
to the colour of a young daughter's room.

I hear hooves lifted and set down again, though
they go nowhere. From the shadows they watch me
with their pink-jelly eyes, their raspberry eyes –
the deer, I mean. The thirsty deer.

In America

The first night I'm driving through upstate New York.
Mile & miles of highway & car beams blinding me.

On the road I'm pursued by the shadows of creatures
from that strange dream I had on the plane.

Orion straddles the black rows of pines
but I'm so far from the land where I left you.

It's 24 hours since our last joint at the lake
where you swam through the reflections of stars.

By gathering those points of light, you were the hunter
who held an entire universe at bay

till I persuaded you to put aside your bow
& into the lake of my mouth

I took each of your belt's three diamonds.
This morning when we woke the grass was wet

& around our bodies were the tracks of constellations
where deer had passed in the night, unnoticed.

Mary Anne MacLeod

(after Carolyn Forché)

What you have heard is true:
I have gone home with the spawning salmon.
Pilgrims through the Turquoise Night,

its Atlantic indigo suns.
No one knows how we do it exactly,
or what guides us back to the river we hatched in

to lay our eggs in soft gravel, and die.
So do I return relentless
until the Isle of Lewis rises like a rocky dawn.

This would have been your kingdom, too:
the salmon, the red deer, the blue hare's
pale shadow, the blue men who live in the Minch –

fallen angels stirring storms against ships.
One of them was your father   oh
    immensity of light and shadow

    light on sea like crumpled tin
    a waterfall on my life's horizon
his blue skin, the sweet smell of heather

Afterwards we lay together
and I thought what kind of son have I created
what kind of son?

You were not born until many years later,
hatched in the gold dust of the West.
My bonny babe, storm-raiser, son of Hell.

If I could, I'd roll the Earth like a stone
back through a life's worth of Novembers.
Unrisen sun, dark oven of sky.

But how my body twists in this
new day: opals and pearls, a hard knowledge.
I have done all I can, my wee man.

I must split to the pink.
A girl's apron dances on a line, a blue man
sinks below the waves.

A red deer lifts its head, a gannet dives.
Salmon leap upstream.

Mar-a-Lago

The water is rising again
though it hasn't rained here for months.

The bayou is coming to the door
of her house, her white colonial house

where she rocks on the porch.
She welcomes the bayou.

The bayou remembers
in the way all swamps remember:

preserving lost centuries
like a jam of clotted green memories.

The woman's dress is ruffled lemon cloth,
a pale froth at her black throat.

The sight of her would put a thirst on you
as you bend in the fields

planting the someday sweetness of sugar.
The sun climbs higher and higher,

a golden elevator to heaven,
while she rocks on the distant porch.

In her lap, a cat sleeps like a gun
on which she rests a ringed hand.

Silver gleam on fur. Later,
when the sun burns down to amber,

she walks to the water's edge
and climbs onto an alligator.

Gliding down the swamp's slow river,
she has nowhere in particular to go.

The dark braid hanging on her back
reminds you suddenly

of that sycamore with its noosey rope
through which you once saw the low sun

like a ruby, as if the earth
was begging you to marry it.

If only you had accepted then,
promising to love its children as your own.

Now it's you who has been forced to kneel
and look, your hands are bleeding.

La Chalupa

Little matchbox, when I picked you up
in a Mexican craft shop in Brooklyn,
I chose you for your image
of a dark-haired woman rowing a canoe.

The canoe is filled with flowers and fruit:
oranges, melons, yellow blooms.
The painted river is decorated with glitter
to suggest how hot the sun must be.

I brought you home as a gift,
watched him turn you over in his fingers
and the woman in the boat watched him
as he slid out your drawer,

took one of the blue-tipped matches,
struck it for his cigarette.
His face glowed in the sudden flare
and the reminder of what love can be:

like yellow flowers;
like light on water; like a woman's
steady gaze; like biting into fruit
below the sun, into the juice and pulp of it.

At a Photography Exhibition in New York Public Library

Below a glass case, men bend their brides backwards to kiss them.
On an altar. On a beach with a cruise ship ghosting the ocean.
On a country lane an old man embraces an old woman.
Hands around waists, bouquets brushing the ground, white lace.

I always knew you'd never bend me backwards
for the first kiss of our married life, never carry me over
the threshold of our home. If we'd walked down the aisle, your bones
would have already been dust, like those in the cold crypts below us.

I would have been the best bride I could for you: diamonds
in my hair, my bridesmaids in primrose, my eyes as bright
as the ring on my finger. But such a day, and its companion life,
was never written in the stars we share. Fellow Aquarian,

what we had is the crystal coffin of something silent, still,
and preserved in what beauty I found there. Read this
and know that at least I imagined. Wherever you are, go
with a bride-thought haunting your shoulder, as lovely as snow.

Rose

I carried one single rose to your home
and when I arrived, you were still at the pub
so your friends and I smoked in the kitchen.

I put the rose in my hair. Roses are best
for a birthday, it was your birthday that night
and the house itself seemed to know it.

A faint shifting of floorboards, a dimming
of the overhead light. A bedroom door bloomed
with a fresh coat of paint

but it was closed. You were late.
We kept drinking. The rose fell out
of my hair. A girl tore at it with her teeth

and then I bit the rose, then there were crushed
petals everywhere. She stuffed them
down my top, then the gin bottle was empty.

You came home with more people.
I gave you the stripped stalk in the hall
outside the closed bedroom door. (The man

I should have given the rose to was passed out
behind it. I should have mentioned that before.)
But it was your birthday, and the rose

was destroyed anyway. You said thank you.
We went into the kitchen. The door
down the hall remained closed. The petals

remained crushed against me. All night I felt
their soft bloody mouths pressed to my breasts,
their last act of love in this world.

Glenveagh

The four of us sat at an iron table
in the courtyard of the castle's café.

I would have poured your tea, a sacred ritual
but in those days the other women

were watching with suspicion.
I sliced a bun in half as if to give you some

then pressed each piece of soft sponge together
along the hairline crack in the glaze.

Back then, for me, love came easy –
like cutting something in two

and showing myself it could be whole again.
Sticky rainbow sprinkles holding lightly

to the blade. I thought love would always run
as red and hot as the tea

I burned my mouth on, as red and hot
as the estate's wild deer that come at dusk

when the tourists have all gone
to lick an empty castle from the water.

Storm Warnings

A woman is coming down my street banging on the doors
of terraced houses. 'Storm warning, storm warning,' she shouts
and throws a handful of flyers at me in the rising wind. Then
she keeps knocking on doors that don't open. From up on the hill
the lighthouse's beacon turns lace curtains red in the windows
and deepens their networks of darkness. I look at the flyers:
STORM WARNING they all say in big writing, so I start
to shove them through letterboxes. A corner shop is all yellow
light below the black sky and I go in to tell people, 'Storm,
there's a storm coming,' and they all hurry away. The guy
at the till says, 'Will I get home in time?' 'I don't know about
that,' I say, 'because it'll hit at half six and already it's quarter
past.' He pulls down the shutters while I go outside, to wind
and red light in every direction. But you could be anywhere
after telling me last night in the snug what you'd never told
anyone. You asked if that changed anything, and I said it didn't
but now I can't find you, and the storm is coming, and it is time
to go inside.

Paris, 13 November 2015

We lie side by side in the street
so it's almost like going to bed
except the night sky is our ceiling, and our blood
has drifted away between cobblestones
like rose petals torn up and scattered.

I don't mind that the last thing I'll see
is a café's *OUVERT* in bright blue and red,
and a neon coffee cup with three white lines
that symbolise rising steam.

Or the lights in your eyes going out –
as if someone turned off the bedside lamp
in your mind – except your eyes are still opening
and opening, and I am frightened.

What were the last things they saw, those eyes?
A cathedral's rose window, or a view
from a tower: grey buildings like rows of soft birds.

My hair on my back as I walked before you
down a flight of stone steps on a hill.
My face turned towards yours, moments ago.

There's a banging like fireworks, but the stars
are as colourless as a window of diamonds.
What we might have dared to think has gone unspoken
and now it always will.

Remember the gig where we had our first kiss?
The world has become as loud as the band
who played that tiny hot bar back in Ireland.

The musicians rolled their eyes and screamed
do ye want more? The drummer played naked.

The singer hated the spotlight on him
and we cheered when he wrenched it down.
How we craved the plunge into darkness,
the careless unscrewing of the moon.

Tropical Ravine House in Belfast Botanic Gardens

Come with me to the Botanic Gardens,
to the crystal house at their heart.

For how many months have I pressed my palms
against your own heart's windows?

Come with me to these
artificial tropics, this simulation of summer.

You are as rare as any shrub
or plant here, in which strange land did you grow?

We are as rich as the ferns, as bright
as the light suffusing from that other world.

Let us never leave but remain, remain, remain,
be as one with the warm air.

Who knows what we might become,
given the time and care?

We have left behind the flags of two countries,
the cafés where each couple shares

a pot of tea and a bun, a wee bun.
I am feeding you such sweet crumbs

between the damp plants.
There are as many purple flowers here

as there are stars in the frozen sky.
But there is only one of you

and this is the only city that I'm from.
You're the sun I've always needed, shining

within our glass home –
and I am home, I am home, I am home.

Eden

Forgive me, Lord, for I have sinned.
In your garden of clear waters and mossy walls
I reached for the high fruit.

With the first crack of breaking skin
and the juice of white flesh in my mouth
I was cast out, and for years now

I've wandered a wasteland.
Barefoot over the glittering dust, below a sky cut
with red wounds of lightning.

I've had a man for every season
since I left you, darling, and I've feasted
on the spices of their open lips:

essence of almond, a strange vanilla,
and biscuits and bread from the oven.
But it was a sin to abandon

your kind arms and simple garden
for men whose faces shone so beautifully
on the stage – who made my veins run

with ecstasy. They were cruel,
and for their love I drank
and drank from the bottomless well.

Still only your face looked back at me
and you said nothing.
These men play me so hard, baby,

like one of their guitars, and I'm just another
face in their crowd, growing older
and pale as the moon.

The river rushes your reflection on
towards the ocean, but you're as still
as the apples hanging like planets

above your quiet world. They cling
pink and tender to their branches
with skins holding close a sweetness

that will always be unknown to them,
which is their own secret selves.

The Cave of Melassini

I carry with me his name etched on a stone
to the lighthouse near Argostoli.

Miniature temple with twenty white pillars,
what can I worship here?

What you warn ships of, I would give myself to:
my body a sunset bleeding over the rocks,

into the grooves of his name.
I want to show him the lemon trees, the rare

Kefalonia violets; to feed him pastries with honey
by the turtle lagoon.

My footprints retreat in the red sand of Xi
but when the sand in the hourglass runs out of time

I'm still praying at Orthodox shrines.
In the underground lake

where the nymph drowned herself
a pebbled bed seems as distant as Ithaca.

Blue and green dream: for the last time her memory
of his back to her as they walked

through the trees; of a time
when she had no fear of snakes in the grass,

or a truck idling under the balcony.
My boatman says the lake's water is both salty

and sweet, freshwater mingling with sea.
I think of her body filling with such strangeness

as she sank through each opal layer
like the world's whispered reminder

there is still much to learn.

Ithaca

One day there will be a morning
when the two of us wake up together.

Padding over tiles in our thick woollen socks,
setting the fire with newspaper twists.

Now they're lighting beacons on the cliffs,
the red signal fires that mean war,

but someday we'll have weak flames
in the grate, the honey of pale sunlit days.

Think of the cast-iron kettle, the small
painted jug filled with flowers;

the tabby cat unlike any other cat
because she will belong to us.

Only a needle will go sailing away
across a vinyl record's black grooves.

And beyond heather fields: the sound
of the ocean, like a vast loom

weaving the waves. My love,
I have seen the future and am not afraid.

Our wanderings will come to an end:
no more the walking of streets

late at night, swallowing half-pearls
that unravel our lives.

No fear of the beautiful goddess
or of the young men who just seem so hungry.

No more will I wait for you, no more
will you fail to come back to me.

I have seen the future through
a cottage window, have been

an unseen ghost trampling the asphodel,
my breath misting the glass.

Oranges

I'll choose for myself next time
who I'll reach out and take
as mine, in the way
I might stand at a fruit stall

having decided
to ignore the apples
the mangoes and kiwis
but hold my hands above

a pile of oranges
as if to warm my skin
before a fire.
Not only have I chosen

oranges, I'll also choose
which orange – I'll test
a few for firmness
scrape some rind off

with my fingernail
so that a citrus scent
will linger there all day.
I won't be happy

with the first one I pick
but will try different ones
until I know you. How
will I know you?

You'll feel warm
between my palms
and I'll cup you like
a handful of holy water.

A vision will come to me
of your exotic land: the sun
you swelled under
the tree you grew from.

A drift of white blossoms
from the orange tree
will settle in my hair
and I'll know.

This is how I will choose
you: by feeling you
smelling you, by slipping
you into my coat.

Maybe then I'll climb
the hill, look down
on the town we live in
with sunlight on my face

and a miniature sun
burning a hole in my pocket.
Thirsty, I'll suck the juice
from it. From you.

When I walk away
I'll leave behind a trail
of lamp-bright rind.

Easter

You walk by holding a bunch of flowers
never knowing that you've just performed a miracle.
Are those flowers for your girl?
I imagine her dressed up like an Easter egg
in yellow and pink. I'd tap at you like an egg,
cracking your thin chocolate shell.
If I were made of chocolate too, I'd break
off parts of myself to give to you and your girl.
Once, I gave my words for *garden*
and *water* and *moonlit* and *love*
to a man who kissed me. After he rolled
a stone over my heart and shut me off
from the world, I had no words left
to describe the dark dream that followed.
Now you've walked by, godlike in jeans
and an old t-shirt, the sun glinting on one
silver earring. Now a rose is once again
not only *rose* but also *soft* and *red*
and *thorn* and *bee* and *honey*.
Now a bird is singing *song* and *tree*
and *nest in a high place* and *blue speckled egg*.
You yourself are glowing with words, they move
up and down you as if they're alive.
The words bring themselves to me
and tell my tongue *sweetness* over and over.
The words are everything. With them,
I'll turn water to wine at your wedding.

Miracle at Standing Rock

(after Eavan Boland)

In Ireland we know the holiness of water:
pooling between green blades in the fields,
resting in marble fonts at church doors.

The grey Atlantic's rise and fall
by Murrisk's Famine ship sculpture,
the rain that people prayed in for hours

when Our Lady appeared to them at Knock.
They said the Rosary over and over,
stringing wet beads through their fingers.

It was 35 years since a poor farmer's spade
birthed our country's first rotting potatoes
from the life-giving ground.

Water cannot cure hunger
or the Choctaw would have drunk their sorrow
as they set out on the Trail of Tears.

But water joins their land to ours,
water that carried the corn that they sent us
though they had so little for themselves.

In some places water itself is a miracle.
You can't drink the black slick of oil
yet it goes on being raised anyway,

like a potato slime that feeds no one.
Why did those potatoes turn? We can't say
for sure. Why did Knock's people pray

hour after hour by a gable wall
and later testify to the Lamb of God, the altar,
the virgin's glittering crown?

That too is uncertain. Fifteen witnesses,
and the one thing their testimonies agreed on
was rain – rain, and the gathering dark.

Why did the English refuse to send food
to Mayo and Galway, why
were the white men afraid of the Ghost Dance?

These are things we share in our stories:
rain and the gathering dark,
our stolen land and our hunger

for miracles. Here is a story
about in which darkness it can best be proved,
the bridge between past and present

that does exist, as both our tribes
have always known! Come, let us eat the lamb,
let its blood replenish the bisonless land.

In its vast silty bed the Missouri finally rests,
as at peace as when it first fell as rain.

The Unicorn Children

I was in my kitchen and it was raining outside.
A strange girl in the garden caught my eye.
She was an Afghan girl, and I thought she looked cold
under the lashing branches and leaves.

I went out to her, and she had three sisters:
all wearing headscarves, and they all had green eyes.
'We are waiting,' they said
and I asked who they were.

For an answer they pulled the scarves from their hair
to reveal in each soft brown forehead
a stubbed velvet horn
then as one they rose as a flock of birds

and flew off. I watched them hover
above the neighbour's house, at the foot of the hill,
before they descended and disappeared.
My mother came to my side and said

'Perhaps they'll be taken care of.'
I shook my head, and went down the road
to the neighbour's yard, where rain made swallowing sounds
on oily water resting in barrels.

I shouted, 'Hello.' There wasn't an answer
and I was turning to go when the back door opened.
One of the girls stumbled out
her mouth gaping soundless

and a rusted sign in the wind screaming for her.
In her forehead was a neat bloody hole.
I ran away and below my feet the road was paved
with giant letters that I couldn't read.

Tigers in Leitrim

My mother calls to tell me there are tigers in Leitrim again.
I say: It's been a thousand years since the last one was killed,
what about the wolves? She says: No wolves yet but I saw the tigers
with my own two eyes, crossing our lawn in the cold milk
of the moon. A tigress and her cubs, who knows what hot dark
and godless enclave they emerged from? I say: Yes, I saw them too.
She says: How? You haven't been home in months. I say: On TV
or whatever, I don't really remember. But the tigers mean something,
I'm sure of it. Why else would they come? She says: Well,
I'm afraid of them. Who knows what strange orbit
they'll travel around our farms and our houses. What about
my lovely hens? I say: Damn your hens. Do me a favour.
Use lipstick to write each of our names on pink scraps of paper,
then let them fall from the window like flowers. She says: And why
would I do that? I say: To tell them. She says: Tell them what?
I say: That we have seen their red shadows taking mouthfuls of dusk
as the sky starts to darken again, and that there are more
of us like them, the only species of cat that loves rain.

Poem for a Friend's Unborn Baby

(for Sadie)

With the turn of the new millennium
we were 10-year-old little witches.
As territorial as our enemy brothers

in the battles we fought to rule the front field,
the back field's silver birches,
each empty stall in the old cow shed.

We were queens
and our crowns were woven
with rushes and daisies and dandelions.

How gold and lovely
we must have seemed,
our war cries rising with the corncrake's call

to Sliabh an Iarainn's lilac mystery –
who could say how many apple trees
grew there? On hazy days

we could barely see the fairy
hill Sheemore's white crucifix
or coaly Arigna's matchstick turbines;

their height and girth and terrible power
then as unfathomable
as the idea of your someday daughter.

Let us raise this glazéd jug
we once dug from Leitrim mud,
and drink from it the river

of ourselves whose source lies in
these hills. Even as the river forks,
so must it remain the same river.

Even when we picked
each autumn's dark and ripening gifts
she was already watching us

with glitter-glue blackberry eyes
unseen in the shadowy ditch.
Will she too know of war?

Will she too wear a daisy crown
till she is captured by boys wielding waterguns,
forced to surrender

and walk home before them
with her hands raised higher
than a mountain cross?

Northern Lights

we were on a train & it was dark beyond the strip of windows
I didn't know what time it was when Muireann said Jesus
look at the moon so we all looked through the glass
agreeing we had never seen a larger whiter rounder more perfect moon
& Emily said this is our time & I thought she meant our time to die
crossing the flat moonlit plain but couldn't ask her to clarify
because a voice cried you can see the northern lights from this side
where the world was NEON   BLUE GREEN   BLUE GREEN
bordered with a lacy crimson glow like the OPEN sign
of the Thai massage parlour high above main street
with its window of old paper lanterns
dusty & dreaming of sky

Cosmic Latte

I have seven sisters, we live in a house
with eight doors. *The colour of space
is a milky beige* says the man on TV

yet if he looked into the eyes of my sisters
he'd see the black of infinity.
All night we drink coffee,

take turns with a kitten's purring universe
on our knees, roll joints and draw
the Milky Way into our lungs

where it meets the stardust
that the man on TV says we're made of.
In this house, each bedroom door

shows a crack of pink light.
Put your eye to it:
you might see whole worlds forming

in cauldrons of matter,
fiery mountains of nebulae,
the aching hole at the heart of it all.

Or just a girl, sleeping,
surrounded by a halo of dust.
Without her, without one tiny piece

of her, without the kitten, without
the weed, things would crumble
and rust. What is the universe made of

if not us? Our voices that fall
as gentle as ash, our cigarettes
burning holes in the sky.

irish coffee

this is how I'll taste
to you: the shock of alcohol
paired with the sweetness of cream
scooped over bitter

silty murk like burnt-
brown fields in winter sunlight.
the air here will leave you dizzy:
drink, it goes down

milk-easy and every
glint of quartz is sugar-precious.

Mercury in Retrograde

Leafy Mercurys drift from the trees
as the sun creeps along the horizon,
in love with humankind.

Autumn is slow and delicious,
turning the river amber and black
in the lights from the bridge.

My blood fills with dust
washed down from the mountains
and every day you're exploring me,

panning for gold.
Who knows what you might find:
rings and chains, old coins,

a single gleaming crown.
For now, there is a night fierce
with galaxies. For now,

you lie by the fire
having already made your fortune.
You'll return home a rich man

and meanwhile I'm listening
to the rush of gold in my veins,
to the oven's hum in the kitchen.

Anything could rise
in the scorched place behind
its yellow square in the darkness,
that lit window in Bethlehem.

Ophelia

We came to meet you, Ophelia.
They said we were reckless, driving down from the city
to that little house in the west.

But we were five women who had nothing
if not each other, and have faced worse things
than your unrest.

On the way we passed sandbags already slung
by the road, long pumps trailing from streams
while the radio said *status red*

and on our phones
all of Ireland a rainbow grid. And us burrowing
straight for the dark violet heart

of things, the sky turning green as a bottle.
A strange light at sea. The air like a balm.
Water folding itself over, settling to glass.

And in the morning we woke to you everywhere.
In the attic, the water tank still gurgled
the house's quiet song

as if a circle of livid trees did not surround us,
as if that low growl rising from the earth
held no fear for us.

Lighting the fire, lighting a joint.
The slither of flames and gentle scrape
of the grinder, turning like a wheel.

The lights in the house all dimming and
coming back. And coming back, and coming back.
As fishing boats drawn up on shingle

would be returned from land, as blue lamps
would re-illuminate the virgin's shrine.
We watched leaves swirl

on the patio, until there were no leaves.
We watched the trees bend and almost break
until the windows were crusted with salt.

Make the world new for us again, Ophelia,
we who won't light cigarettes from a candle
for the sake of a sailor's soul –

despite what we have borne
at the hands of sailors. Oh tropical storm.
This is no country of palm trees and flower-

filled ditches, but it is the only land we know.
Women who dream of the impossible,
our roots grow deep.

Amongst Women

I

I was born on the Falls Road, near a mural of Bobby Sands.
Oh Bobby, no one wants us,
only the painted versions of ourselves.

I am naked, he stripped me naked,
does my naked body mean nothing to you?
Why do ye all remain friends with these men?
Father forgive them, they know not what they do.

He too threw flowers before you, Bobby,
my god for whom I killed every baby boy in our kingdom,
slaughtered every flock in the fields,
turned oceans to the colour of sacrifice.

Now the lights of shipping lanes are all put out,
the beacon's cinder fades up on the cliff.

Now my baby trembles on the brink of birth
in the current where river joins sea
like two bodies that once joined as night came on,
stars going off like tiny bombs.

There's a shadow coming with the moon,
a slowly spreading stain across the earth.
Oh Sea of Tranquillity, oh Marsh of Decay.
Oh Bay of Rainbows, oh Ocean of Storms.

II

I become thin when you leave, as if you sucked the flesh from me
so I'd finally fit the clothes you always imagined me in.
My heart's all foam, like the white wake that follows the boat home.
But I can't return, for I ate the six seeds you gave me
here in this city and now you are gone. I eat nothing but stones.
I am thin. It is winter. My blood tastes air, but this is no harvest sacrifice.
The ground it stains is barren and knows no rain.

III

For what died the sons of Róisín was it this?
Rolling grass seed and bog cotton into a spliff,
breathing the names of my townlands back into my self:
Red Marsh, Black Wood, Small Watery Place,
Raised Land of the Fox, Round Hill of the Lights,
Yellow Hill Ridge, the Lone Bush of Martin,
Back Hill of the Young Calves, Round Hill of the Boys.
Go west, young woman, return to a time
when you were only light and water, water and light –

IV

Still, love rises in me like water:
a forest's dark holy well.
I've been to such places, knelt
by their damp mossy steps.
I've seen the wordless tokens
left there by people: coins, shells, beads
and the silent ghosts
of red rags tied to the trees.

V

Amongst women, I wait on the shore
of our twilight world, with its threat of storms always.
Stripped naked, we shield little candles
with our hands: prayers for salvation, or a funeral offering.

Now we see the lonely road, footprints on the frozen plain
where many have gone before, all bearing their own
vessels and trying out a thousand different words for *snow*
but their voices fade and each of us
must find our own way.

I collect melting ice, rivulets escaping west, in a vessel
that will be my only child. The pale gauze
of northern lights, a wedding veil;
the stars, my indifferent gods.

Hail Mary, full of grace. Our Lord is with thee.
Blessed art thou amongst women,
and blessed is the fruit of thy womb, Jesus.
Holy Mary, Mother of God, pray for us sinners
now and at the hour of our death.

Wedding Below the Perseid Meteor Shower

I wear a blue dress, my bridesmaids are all in white.
Our wedding cake has birthday cake candles,
little nostalgias of wax. The cake itself we cut up
and parcel in tinfoil, handing it out to our guests.
All we ask of them is to wait until the apocalypse
before they defrost it, pick off the sweet icing,
and throw out the rest. Meanwhile, you'll find me
and my husband with cardboard signs
round our necks to inform you THE END IS NIGH.
It will be a different kind of marriage this time,
that between mortal bodies and the fatal love
of a meteor or a nuclear bomb. But back to our first,
original wedding in which we walk up the aisle
between our family and friends, and everyone
is so happy for us. The service is short and religious.
The priest reads the parable I heard as a child,
about the virgins who forgot oil for their lamps
and were shut out of heaven. Leaving the church,
we walk into an ash of volcanic confetti.
The train of my veil snakes behind me
like a comet's tail of old ice and stardust, on its way
to the red heat of a marriage bed.

Tuam

At Choeung Ek, our guide points out
the sugar palm's serrated leaves –
good for cutting throats. In these fields

a tree can be a knife. A mouth
that knew only several joyful tastes
of what should have been a lifetime's sugar

can now be a jawbone
separated from its tiny skull.
In times of heavy rain, bones and teeth

and scraps of clothing surface
in the mud – our guide requests we do
not touch them. It is as if,

he says, the dead will not rest. This
was once an orchard, watermelon grove.
Now the land swells gently where

the mass graves are, like the stipple
of our lazy beds that predate the Famine.
Here, the sun rises like an apple

red and whole. I reach out to
the coloured bracelets hanging on
the Killing Tree. Here, a tree can hold

for decades the brain-bone-fragments
left by babies' heads. Our guide
says look, but I do not want to look.

Sunlight touches the
unstirring lake, the stupa's dusty glass
behind which 5,000 skulls

gaze back at us, incurious.
For years the only sounds that reached them
in the dark were of birds

and monkeys calling to their young,
calls passed down through generations.
One century before

a Galway field's bone-chamber
was found by two young boys
the missionaries who first came to Angkor

said the jungle temple was so strange
and ancient they did not believe
the natives capable of building it.

Granuaile

I have sailed all night through the storm.
On the cliff, the lighthouse warns my ship to stay away.

Do I go forwards, can I turn back?
At Caherciveen I disembark on tar-black sand,
where the tide becomes nothing and nothing.

For miles along the shore it leaves me babies
with thin wet limbs and the liquid eyes of aliens.

I find them by their failing hearts,
which beat as dim red lamps in each translucent body
and edge their beds of foam with fire.

I have pulled dead women from the water,
carried to my boat each naked corpse subdued and happy
like a new wife.

What god has brought together, let no man separate.
Radio voices crackle and vanish,
naming where they'll wait for me:

Audley Cove. Belfast. Achill Island. Rosses Point.
Horse Island. Louisburgh. Cape Clear. Holyhead.

Bones of my bones, flesh of my flesh.
For what died the sons of Róisín was it this?

Beware, beware, the unseen ship, the revolver at my hip.
I will sail between the setting of the sun
and the rising of the bone-white moon

until even the familiar stars will show no mercy.
I know every rock and twisted cove that marks
this barren place. I know my way in the dark.

Notes

Tom Barry (12): Tom Barry was a guerrilla leader in the Irish Republican Army, commanding the West Cork Brigade's flying column during the Irish War of Independence (1919-1921).

Mary Anne MacLeod (23): Mary Anne Trump, *née* MacLeod, was the mother of Donald Trump, 45th President of the United States of America. Born in 1912, she was a Gaelic speaker from the Isle of Lewis off the west coast of Scotland and emigrated to New York at the age of 18.

Miracle at Standing Rock (44): The village of Knock in Ireland became a Catholic pilgrimage sight after 15 people claimed that on the wet evening of August 21, 1879, they collectively witnessed an apparition of Our Lady, Saint Joseph, Saint John the Evangelist, and Jesus Christ (represented by an altar with a cross and a lamb) on the gable wall of the local church.

Standing Rock is a Native American reservation in North Dakota and South Dakota on which President Trump approved the completion of a crude oil pipeline that runs through sacred lands and could contaminate the Standing Rock Sioux's drinking water. In 2017 thousands of indigenous and environmental protestors were evicted from the site in a military-style takeover.

Cosmic Latte (51): Cosmic Latte is the name given to a beigeish white that was determined to be the average colour of the universe by a team of astronomers from Johns Hopkins University.

Tuam (60): A mass grave at former Bon Secours Mother and Baby Home in Tuam, Co. Galway, underwent an initial excavation after local historian Catherine Corless published research indicating that a structure once used as a sewage tank contains the bodies of children and babies. The 'substantial quantity' of human remains discovered in the structure have not yet been identified, and more excavations are necessary in order to recover the rest. There are no burial records for almost 800 children who died at the home.

Choeung Ek is the most infamous of Cambodia's 'Killing Fields', which is the name given to the sites at which the Khmer Rouge regime murdered over one million people between 1975 and 1979 before burying them in mass graves that have remained largely untouched.

Granuaile (62): Gráinne Ní Mháille – known colloquially as Granuaile – was a 16th-century chieftain of the Ó Máille dynasty. Basing herself out of her castle on Clare Island, and with several hundred men at her command, she earned the reputation of 'Pirate Queen' due to her attacks on ships passing along the west coast of Ireland, which was then under British rule.